Rabbit

Nicole Boswell

Rabbits have long ears.

Wild rabbits are usually brown.

They have strong back legs to jump far.

Rabbits live in holes in the ground.

Rabbits stand on their back legs to look out for danger.

Rabbits eat grass and plants.

ears

eye

nose

tail